Your first 100 words in

CHINESE

MANDARIN

Beginner's Quick & Easy Guide to Demystifying Greek Script

Series concept
Jane Wightwick

Illustrations
Mahmoud Gaafar

Chinese edition
Chen Ji

McGraw Hill

New York Chicago San Francisco Lisbon London Madrid Mexico City
Milan New Delhi San Juan Seoul Singapore Sydney Toronto

Audio CD edition
The accompanying CD contains three tracks for each topic:

Repeat and Remember
Speak and Understand
Test Yourself

Topics: 1 Around the House (tracks 2–4), 2 Clothes (tracks 5–7) 3 Around Town (tracks 8–10), 4 Countryside (tracks 11–13), 5 Opposites (tracks 14–16), 6 Animals (tracks 17–19), 7 Parts of the Body (tracks 20–22), 8 Useful Expressions (tracks 23–25), Round-Up (tracks 26–29)

1 2 3 4 5 6 7 8 9 10 11 12 13 14 15 16 17 18 19 20   VLP/VLP   0 9 8 7

ISBN 978-0-8442-2397-1 (book)
MHID   0-8442-2397-2 (book)

ISBN 978-0-07-149879-1 (book & CD set)
MHID   0-07-149879-6 (book & CD set)

ISBN 978-0-07-149880-7 (book part of set)
MHID   0-07-149880-X (book part of set)

McGraw-Hill books are available at special quantity discounts to use as premiums and sales promotions, or for use in corporate training programs. For more information, please write to the Director of Special Sales, Professional Publishing, McGraw-Hill, Two Penn Plaza, New York, NY 10121-2298. Or contact your local bookstore.

Other titles in this series

Your First 100 Words in Arabic
Your First 100 Words in Arabic, CD edition
Your First 100 Words in French
Your First 100 Words in German
Your First 100 Words in Greek
Your First 100 Words in Greek, CD edition
Your First 100 Words in Hebrew
Your First 100 Words in Hindi
Your First 100 Words in Italian
Your First 100 Words in Japanese
Your First 100 Words in Korean
Your First 100 Words in Korean, CD edition
Your First 100 Words in Pashto
Your First 100 Words in Persian
Your First 100 Words in Russian
Your First 100 Words in Spanish
Your First 100 Words in Spanish, CD edition
Your First 100 Words in Urdu, CD edition
Your First 100 Words in Vietnamese

This book is printed on acid-free paper.

◎ CONTENTS

○ INTRODUCTION

In this activity book you'll find 100 key words for you to learn to read in Chinese. All of the activities are designed specifically for reading non-Latin script languages. Many of the activities are inspired by the kind of games used to teach children to read their own language: flashcards, matching games, memory games, joining exercises, etc. This is not only a more effective method of learning to read a new script, but also much more fun.

We've included a **Scriptbreaker** to get you started. This is a friendly introduction to the Chinese characters that will give you tips on how to remember the letters.

Then you can move on to the eight **Topics**. Each topic presents essential words in large type. There is also a pronunciation guide so you know how to say the words. These words are also featured in the tear-out **Flashcard** section at the back of the book. When you've mastered the words, you can go on to try out the activities and games for that topic.

There's also a **Round-up** section to review all your new words and the **Answers** to all the activities to check yourself.

Follow this 4-step plan for maximum success:

1 Have a look at the key topic words with their pictures. Then tear out the flashcards and shuffle them. Put them Chinese side up. Try to remember what the word means and turn the card over to check with the English. When you can do this, cover the pronunciation and try to say the word and remember the meaning by looking at the Chinese characters only.

2 Put the cards English side up and try to say the Chinese word. Try the cards again each day both ways around. (When you can remember a card for seven days in a row, you can file it.)

3 Try out the activities and games for each topic. This will reinforce your recognition of the key words.

4 After you have covered all the topics, you can try the activities in the **Round-up** section to test your knowledge of all the 100 words in the book. You can also try shuffling all the flashcards together to see how many you can remember.

This flexible and fun way of reading your first words in Chinese should give you a head start whether you're learning at home or in a group.

◎ SCRIPTBREAKER

The purpose of this Scriptbreaker is to introduce you to Chinese characters and how they are used. You should not try to memorize the characters at this stage, nor try to form them yourself. Instead, have a quick look through this section and then move on to the topics, glancing back if you want to work out the characters in a particular word. Remember, though, that recognizing the whole shape of the word in an unfamiliar script is just as important as knowing how it is made up. Using this method you will have a much more instinctive recall of vocabulary and will gain the confidence to expand your knowledge in other directions.

Chinese particularly suits this visual approach since the written language is not composed of individual letters of an alphabet, but of a series of ideograms, or "characters." This is often perceived as an added difficulty for a learner, but there is also a positive aspect. There is no alphabet to memorize and, by connecting particular characters to their meaning and pronunciation, you can start steadily to build up a basic vocabulary from day one. It is generally thought that with 1,200 to 1,500 characters you can understand the gist of a Chinese newspaper and these first 100 words will show you that this is an achievable goal.

Chinese characters evolved out of pictograms used as a writing system by primitive hunters. A few characters still resemble the object or concept they refer to, but most have changed beyond recognition. The complete set of characters was simplified by the People's Republic of China (PRC) and both the number and complexity of the characters were reduced. Although the original "traditional" characters are still used in some parts of the Chinese-speaking world, the simplified characters are the most common, and this is the system used in this book. The pronunciation is given in the Mandarin dialect, again the most widespread and the official dialect of the PRC.

◎ One character words

Some words, particularly basic vocabulary, consist of a single character. Others are a combination of two or more characters.

A few characters still bear a visual relation to their meaning:

mountain 山 *shan*

door 门 *men*

big 大 *da*

small 小 *xiao*

However, most characters no longer bear any discernable relation to their meaning:

monkey 猴 *hou*

bed 床 *chuang*

shoe 鞋 *xie*

Some characters look similar to each other and you will have to pay special attention to telling the difference between them:

lake 湖 *hu*

river 河 *he*

sea 海 *hai*

Try to identify the common elements (in the above case the first part of the character, meaning "water") and concentrate on the differences.

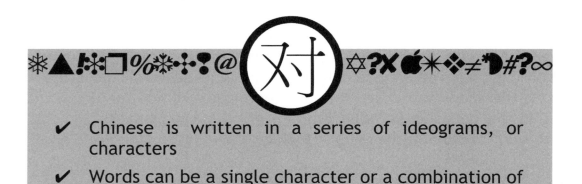

✔ Chinese is written in a series of ideograms, or characters

✔ Words can be a single character or a combination of two or more characters

◎ Multi-character words

When you begin to look at the topics, you will notice that the majority of the 100 words are made up of two or more characters in combination. In its simplest form, these combinations can often help you to understand the word. If you know any, or all, of the characters making up a word, you may be able to guess at the meaning of the combination.

Chinese is a very literal language and this can also help you as a learner. Often where we would use a single word in English, Chinese will use a combination. For example, several of the words in the first topic, begin with the character 电 (*dian*) meaning "electric":

telephone 电话 *dian-hua* ("electric speaking")

television 电视机 *dian-shi-ji* ("electric watching machine")

refrigerator 电冰箱 *dian-bing-xiang* ("electric ice-box")

computer 电脑 *dian-nao* ("electric brain")

Concepts such as "big" and "small" are also used a lot in combination:

mouse 小鼠 *xiao-shu* ("small rat")

coat 大衣 *da-yi* ("big jacket")

Look for the common elements in these combinations since they can give you a lifeline. For example, once you know the word for car, or "vehicle":

汽车 *qi-che*

you are half-way to knowing the words for bus and taxi:

bus 公共汽车 *gong-gong-qi-che* ("public vehicle")

taxi 出租车 *chu-zu-che* ("vehicle for hire")

However, be aware that this literal system does not always work and sometimes characters will combine to produce a different meaning from what you might expect.

✔ Many words are made up of two of more characters
✔ You will find common characters in related words which can help you to guess at the meaning

◎ Pronunciation tips

Chinese words consist of syllables rather than individual letter sounds. The pronunciation in this book is written in the standard Pinyin transcription familiar to most Chinese speakers. Some of the sounds are familiar but here are some tips for pronouncing the more unfamiliar elements:

x a Pinyin "x" is pronounced as "sh" as in "<u>sh</u>eep"

z a Pinyin "z" is pronounced as "ds" as in "ki<u>ds</u>"

q a Pinyin "q" is similar to "ch" as in "<u>ch</u>ildren"

zh is pronounced like "dr" as in "<u>dr</u>ove"

r is pronounced with the tip of the tongue turned up and back

h is pronounced like "ch" in the Yiddish word "chutzpah"

ü is an "u" pronounced with rounded lips as in the German "für"

Note that vowels are pronounced separately in Chinese. So *xie* (shoe) should be pronounced "shee-eh."

◎ Tones

Chinese is a tonal language. Every syllable in Chinese has its own tone. Putonghua (or Mandarin Chinese) has four distinct tones (five if the neutral tone is included): 1st tone, high and level; 2nd tone, rising; 3rd tone, falling-rising; 4th tone, falling. This means that syllables which are pronounced the same but have different tones will mean different things. All of the four tones fall within the natural voice range. You don't have to have a particular type of voice to speak Chinese.

These tone marks can be written in Pinyin over the main vowel of a syllable. Although the tones are important, it takes time to master them and using the tone marks does not help much in the early stages of learning Chinese. However, the context will help you to be understood even if your pronunciation is not perfect. After the elementary stage, for which this programme is designed, you can be more confident about embarking on the task of achieving perfection in pronouncing the correct tone(s) associated with each of the characters, as well as learning to form the basic Chinese characters for yourself.

✔ Spoken Chinese is made up of syllables pronounced with different tones

✔ The Pinyin transcription given in this will help you start to connect a character to its pronunciation

❶ AROUND THE HOME

Look at the pictures of things you might find in a house.
Tear out the flashcards for this topic.
Follow steps 1 and 2 of the plan in the introduction.

桌子
zhuo-zi

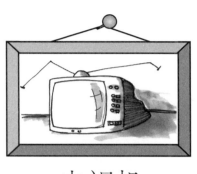

电视机
dian-shi-ji

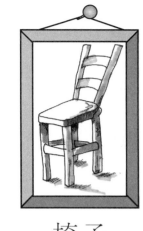

窗户
chuang-hu

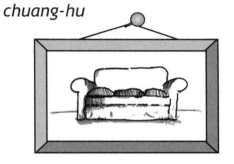

椅子
yi-zi

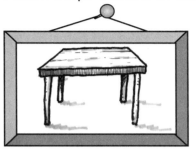

电脑
dian-nao

电话
dian-hua

沙发 *sha-fa*

床 *chuang*

电冰箱
dian-bing-xiang

橱柜
chu-gui

炉子
lu-zi

门
men

9

◎ **M**atch the pictures with the words, as in the example.

沙发
床
窗户
桌子
电视机
电脑
电话
椅子

◎ **N**ow match the Chinese household words to the English.

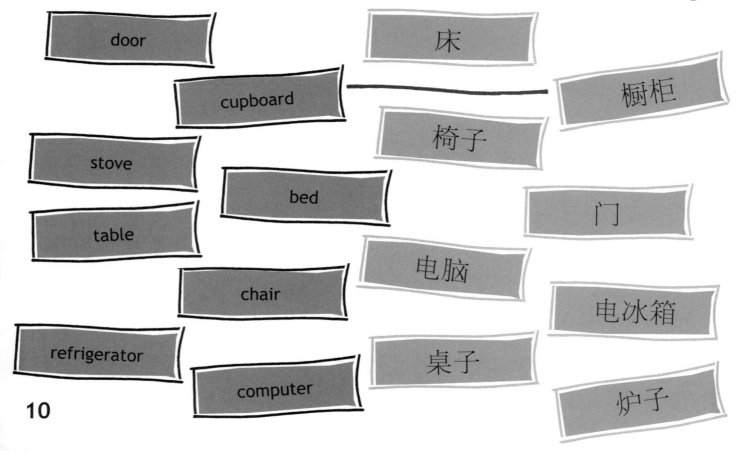

door   床

cupboard   橱柜

              椅子

stove

              bed   门

table

              电脑

              chair   电冰箱

refrigerator

              computer   桌子

                           炉子

◎ **M**atch the words and their pronunciation.

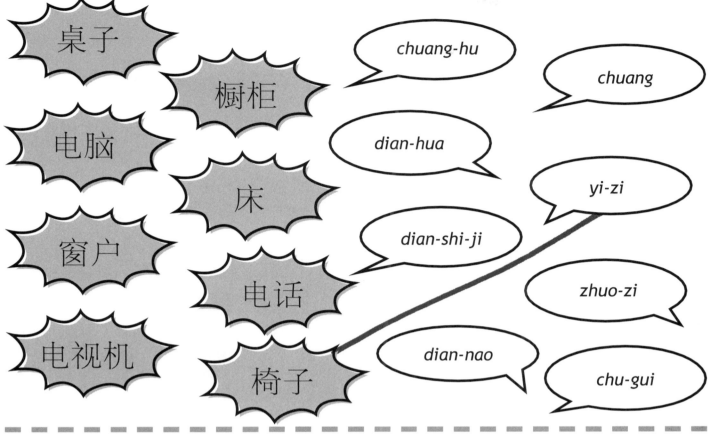

桌子
橱柜
电脑
床
窗户
电话
电视机
椅子

chuang-hu
chuang
dian-hua
yi-zi
dian-shi-ji
zhuo-zi
dian-nao
chu-gui

◎ **S**ee if you can find these words in the word square.

The words can run left to right, or top to bottom:

炉子
床
椅子
电冰箱
门
沙发

自	电	冰	箱	车	衣	橱	连
猫	狗	便	车	电	耳	朵	干
沙	车	牛	床	箱	贵	橱	汽
发	电	大	车	自	柜	椅	公
橱	桥	子	冈	重	田	子	头
马	重	林	指	再	森	自	晴
了	炉	子	这	场	重	鱼	行
场	头	眼	再	手	门	花	车

Decide where the household items should go. Then write the correct number in the picture, as in the example.

1. 桌子
2. 椅子
3. 沙发
4. 电视机
5. 电话
6. 床
7. 橱柜
8. 炉子
9. 电冰箱
10. 电脑
11. 窗户
12. 门

◎ **N**ow see if you can fill in the household word at the bottom of the page by choosing the correct Chinese.

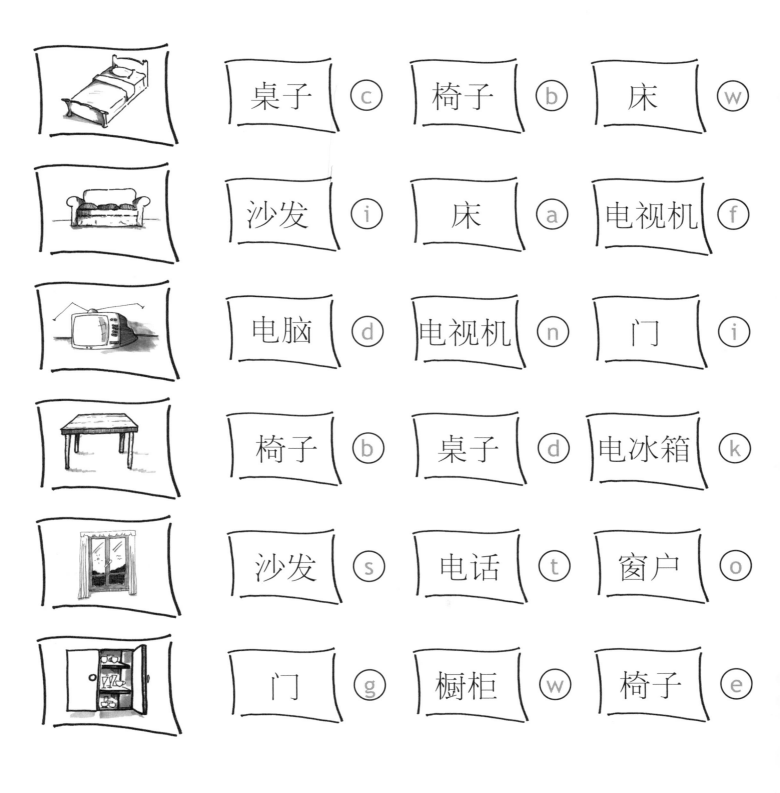

桌子 (c)   椅子 (b)   床 (w)

沙发 (i)   床 (a)   电视机 (f)

电脑 (d)   电视机 (n)   门 (i)

椅子 (b)   桌子 (d)   电冰箱 (k)

沙发 (s)   电话 (t)   窗户 (o)

门 (g)   橱柜 (w)   椅子 (e)

English word: (w) ( ) ( ) ( ) ( ) ( )

② CLOTHES

Look at the pictures of different clothes.
Tear out the flashcards for this topic.
Follow steps 1 and 2 of the plan in the introduction.

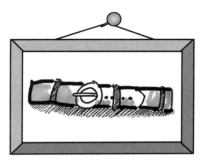

皮带
pi-dai

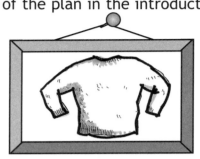

毛衣
mao-yi

短裤
duan-ku

裤子
ku-zi

袜子
wa-zi

T-恤衫
ti-xü-shan

大衣
da-yi

裙子
qün-zi

连衣裙
lian-yi-qün

帽子 *mao-zi*

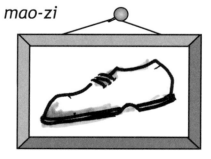

鞋 *xie*

衬衫 *chen-shan*

◎ **M**atch the Chinese words and their pronunciation.

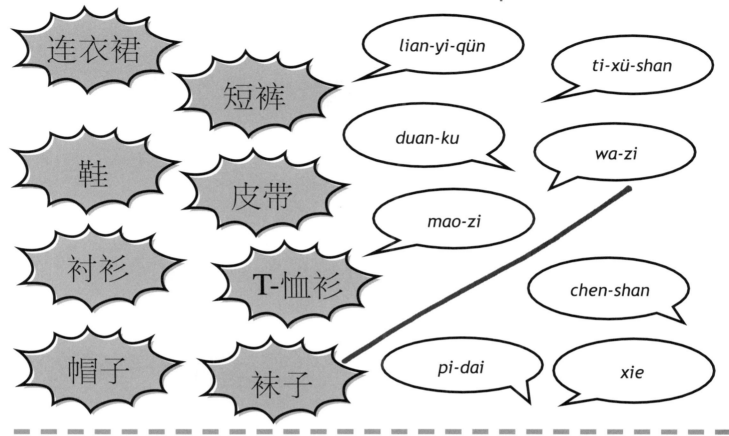

◎ **S**ee if you can find these clothes in the word square.

The words can run left to right, or top to bottom:

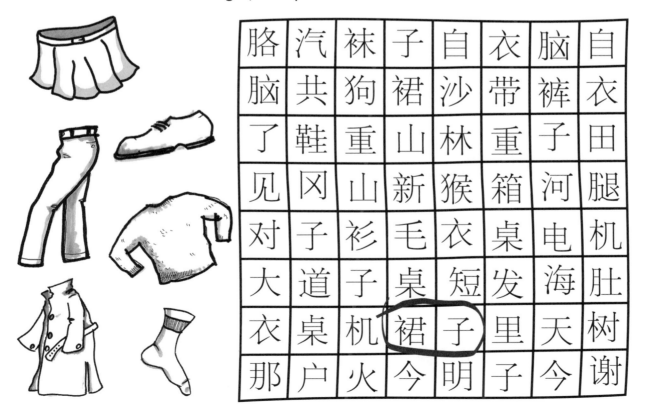

◎ **N**ow match the Chinese words, their pronunciation, and the English meaning, as in the example.

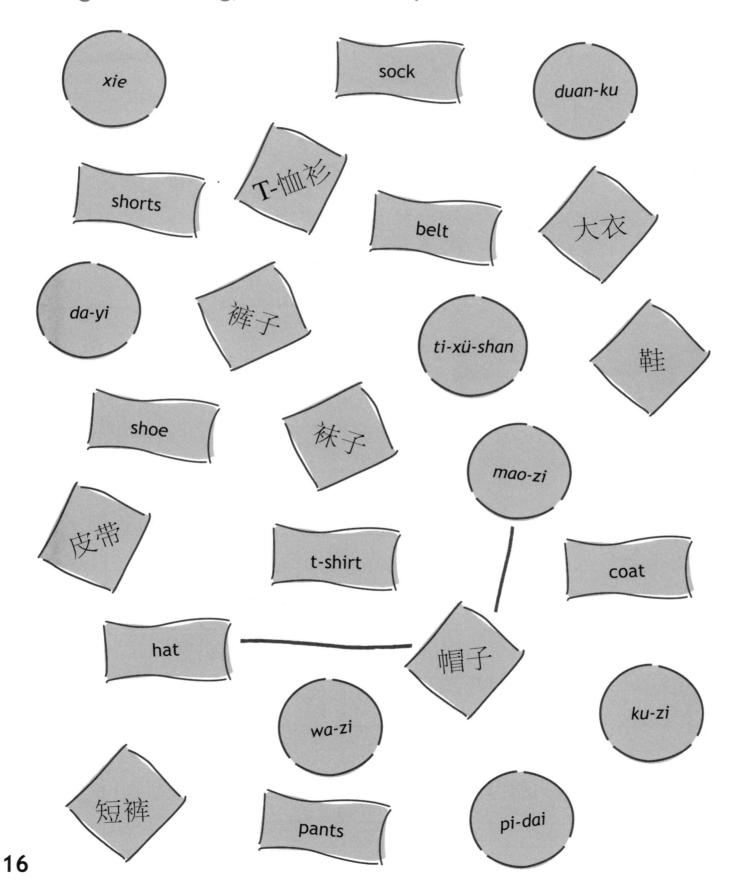

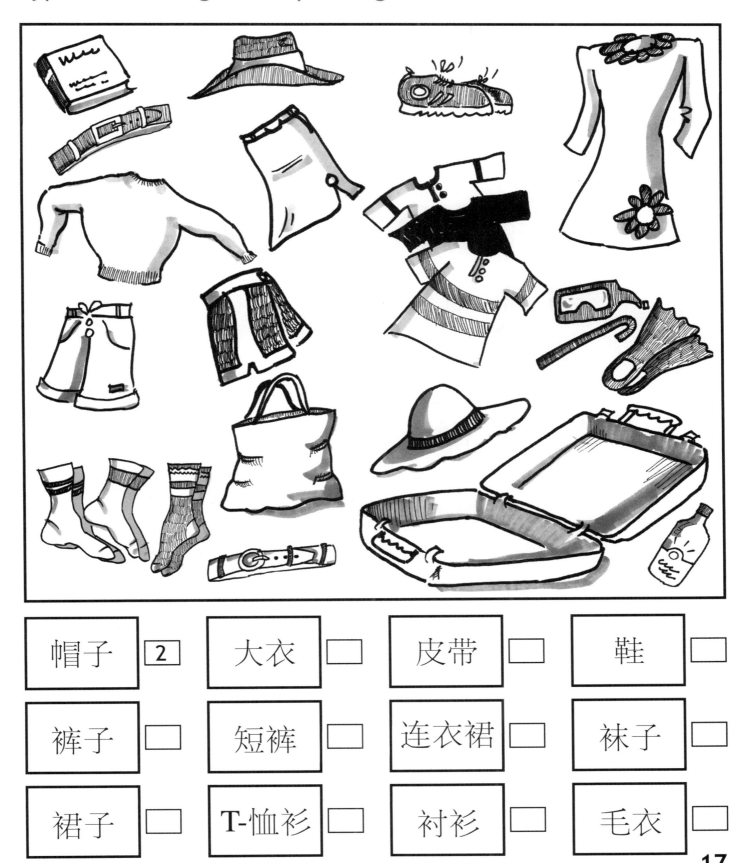

○ **C**andy is going on vacation. Count how many of each type of clothing she is packing in her suitcase.

帽子	2	大衣	☐	皮带	☐	鞋	☐
裤子	☐	短裤	☐	连衣裙	☐	袜子	☐
裙子	☐	T-恤衫	☐	衬衫	☐	毛衣	☐

17

Someone has ripped up the Chinese words for clothes.
Can you join the two halves of the words, as the example?

❸ AROUND TOWN

Look at the pictures of things you might around town.
Tear out the flashcards for this topic.
Follow steps 1 and 2 of the plan in the introduction.

饭店 *fan-dian*

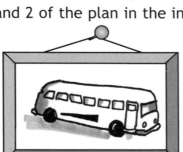
公共汽车
gong-gong-qi-che

房子
fang-zi

汽车
qi-che

电影院
dian-ying-yuan

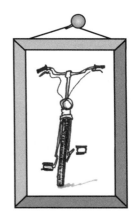
自行车
zi-xing-che

火车
huo-che

出租车 *chu-zu-che*

学校 *xüe-xiao*

道路 *dao-lu*

商店 *shang-dian*

餐馆
can-guan

19

◎ **M**atch the Chinese words to their English equivalents.

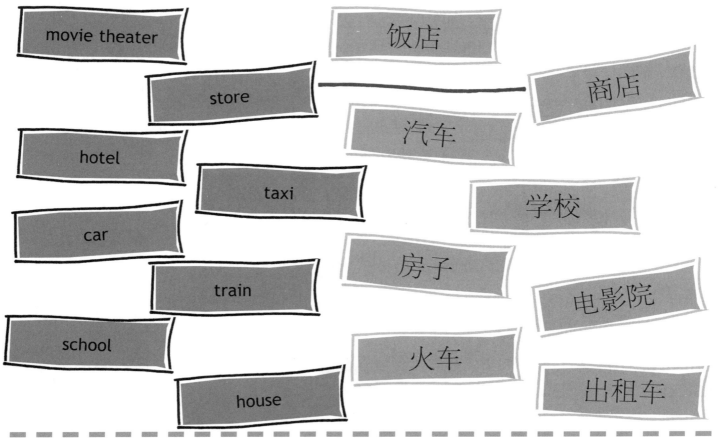

movie theater	饭店
store	商店
hotel	汽车
taxi	学校
car	房子
train	电影院
school	火车
house	出租车

◎ **N**ow list the correct order of the English words to match the Chinese word chain, as in the example.

公共汽车 — 房子 — 道路 — 自行车 — 汽车 — 火车 — 出租车

bicycle   taxi   house   train   bus   road   car

4 ___ ___ ___ ___ ___ ___

◎ **M**atch the words to the signs.

学校　　　汽车　　　自行车　　　公共汽车

餐馆　　　火车　　　饭店　　　出租车

◎ **N**ow choose the Chinese word that matches the picture to fill in the English word at the bottom of the page.

出租车 c	汽车 f	房子 s
道路 c	学校 a	公共汽车 k
火车 h	汽车 e	餐馆 u
房子 b	自行车 o	火车 w
学校 o	道路 h	饭店 s
饭店 r	商店 g	电影院 l

English word: s ◯ ◯ ◯ ◯ ◯

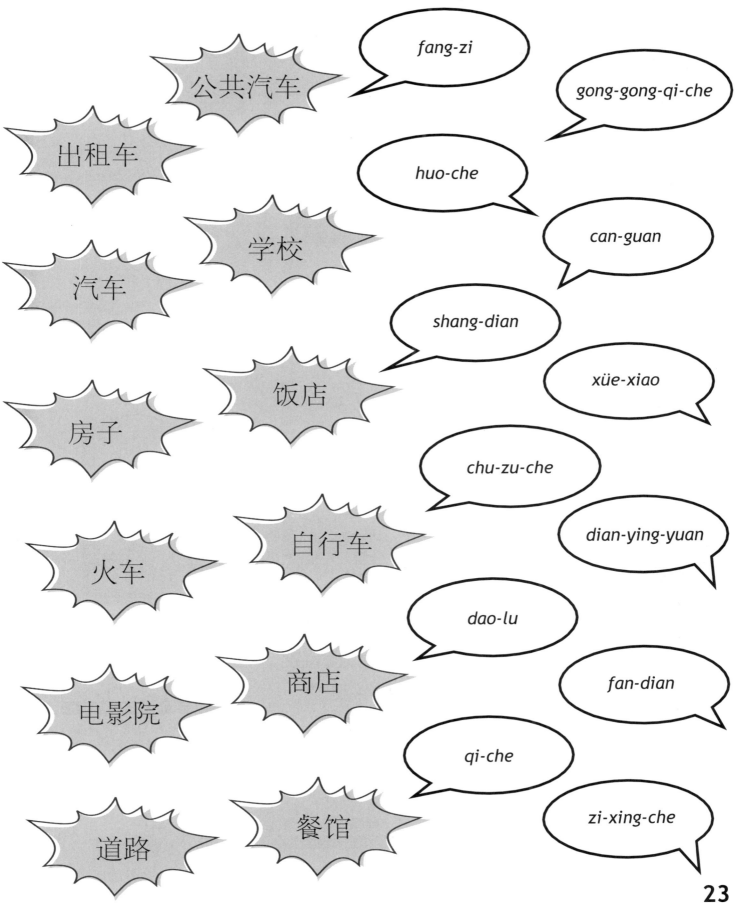

④ COUNTRYSIDE

Look at the pictures of things you might find in the countryside.
Tear out the flashcards for this topic.
Follow steps 1 and 2 of the plan in the introduction.

山冈
shan-gang

桥 *qiao*

农场
nong-chang

山 *shan*

湖
hu

树 *shu*

河 *he*

海 *hai*

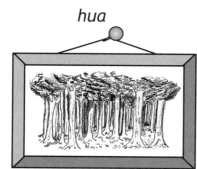

花
hua

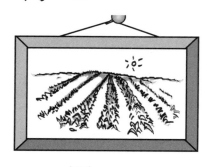

田 *tian*

沙漠
sha-mo

森林
sen-lin

Can you match all the countryside words to the pictures.

山
农场
海
森林
沙漠
山冈
湖
桥
河
花
树
田

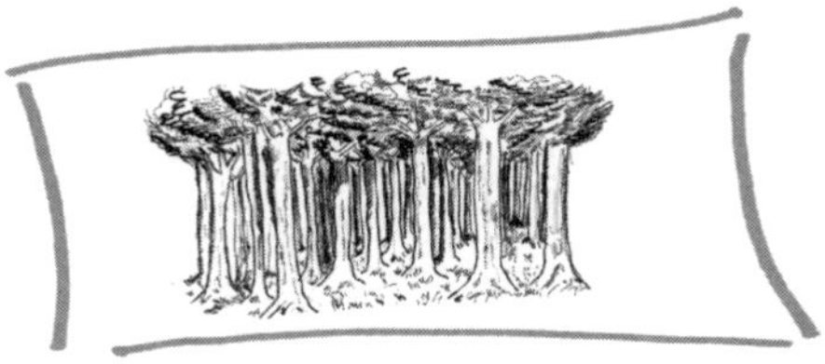

◎ **N**ow check (✔) the features you can find in this landscape.

桥	✔	树	☐	沙漠	☐	山冈	☐
山	☐	海	☐	田	☐	森林	☐
湖	☐	河	☐	花	☐	农场	☐

◎ **M**atch the Chinese words and their pronunciation.

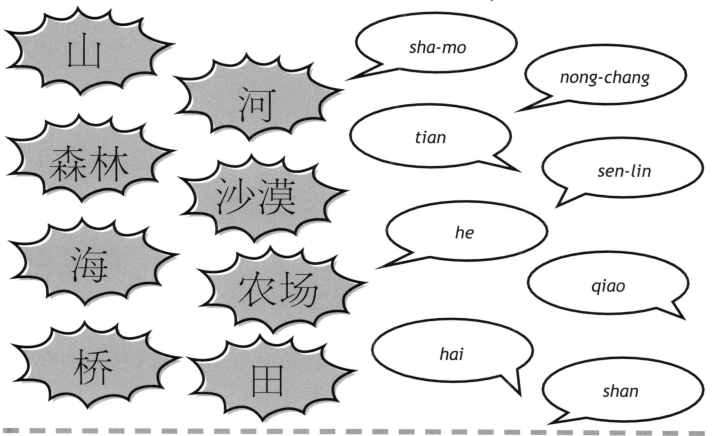

- -

◎ **S**ee if you can find these words in the word square.

The words can run left to right, or top to bottom.

树
农场
山冈
花
桥
湖

公	大	饭	膊	橱	牛	车	宜
自	山	冈	行	脑	车	背	脊
田	象	了	鱼	门	农	森	快
帽	头	湖	狗	好	场	花	鸭
花	冈	狮	马	鼻	猴	房	旧
河	慢	鞋	道	恤	裙	河	请
羊	哪	树	天	窗	今	电	里
明	机	谢	车	那	明	谢	桥

27

◎ **F**inally, test yourself by joining the Chinese words, their pronunciation, and the English meanings, as in the example.

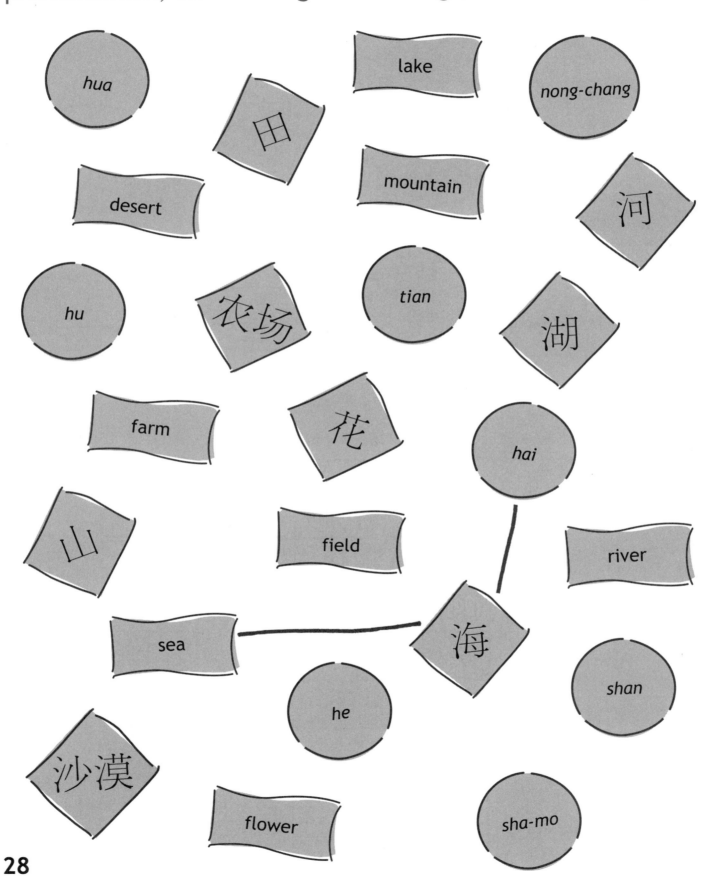

Look at the pictures.
Tear out the flashcards for this topic.
Follow steps 1 and 2 of the plan in the introduction.

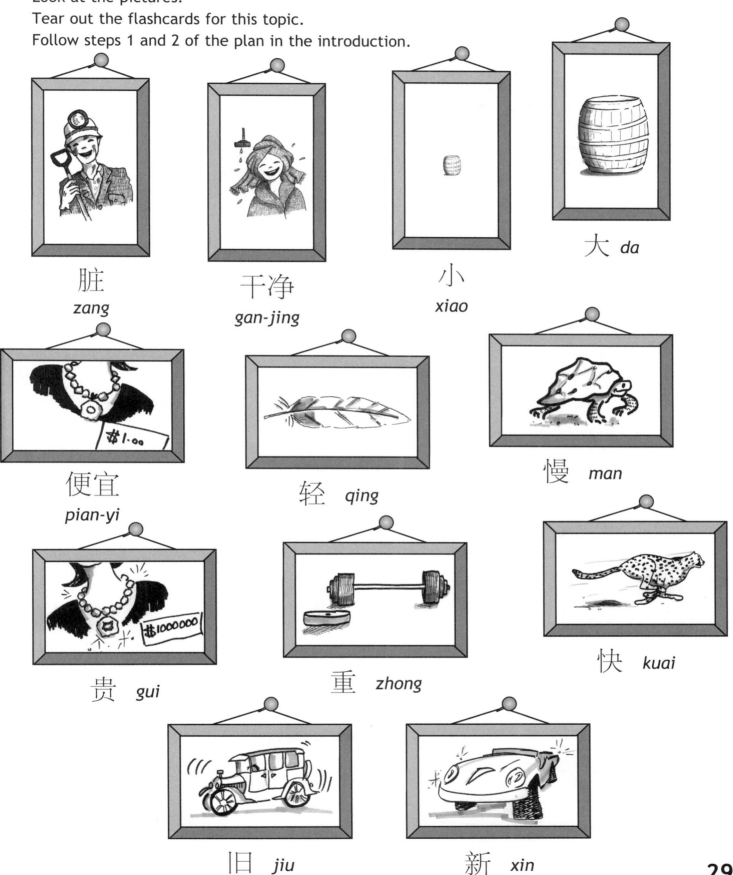

脏
zang

干净
gan-jing

小
xiao

大 *da*

便宜
pian-yi

轻 *qing*

慢 *man*

贵 *gui*

重 *zhong*

快 *kuai*

旧 *jiu*

新 *xin*

⊚ Join the Chinese words to their English equivalents.

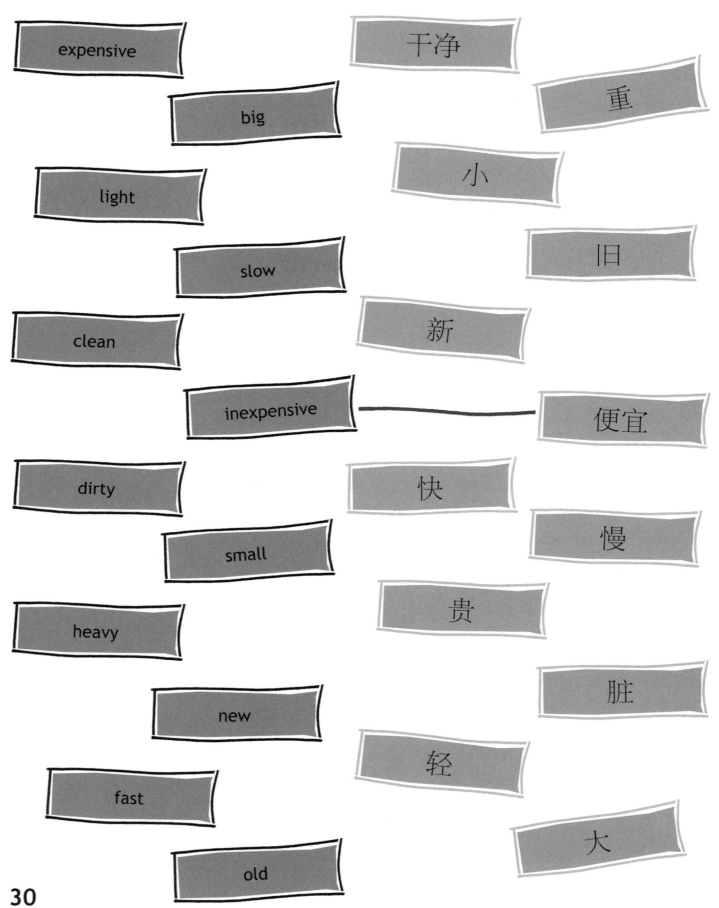

expensive

干净

重

big

小

light

旧

slow

新

clean

inexpensive —————— 便宜

dirty

快

慢

small

贵

heavy

脏

new

轻

fast

大

old

Now choose the Chinese word that matches the picture to fill in the English word at the bottom of the page.

快 ⓒ	慢 ⓣ	干净 ⓗ
新 ⓓ	便宜 ⓐ	脏 ⓗ
大 ⓡ	重 ⓐ	小 ⓤ
贵 ⓟ	便宜 ⓝ	新 ⓞ
新 ⓖ	轻 ⓒ	小 ⓢ
干净 ⓜ	旧 ⓝ	慢 ⓔ

English word: ○ ○ ○ ○ ○ ○

F ind the odd one out in these groups of words.

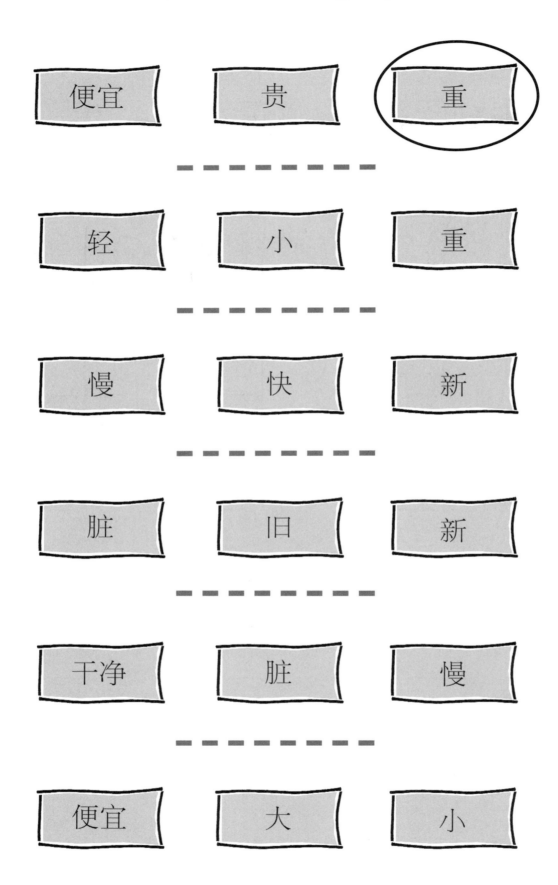

便宜　　贵　　重

轻　　小　　重

慢　　快　　新

脏　　旧　　新

干净　　脏　　慢

便宜　　大　　小

Finally, join the English words to their Chinese opposites, as in the example.

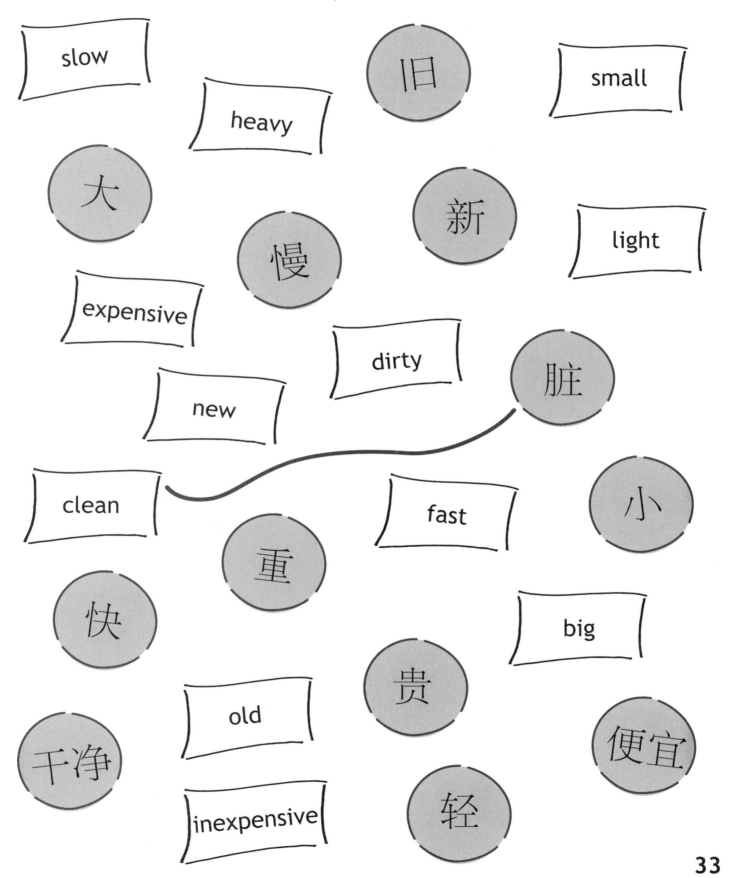

slow

heavy

旧

small

大

新

慢

light

expensive

dirty

脏

new

clean

fast

小

重

快

big

old

贵

干净

便宜

inexpensive

轻

6 ANIMALS

Look at the pictures.
Tear out the flashcards for this topic.
Follow steps 1 and 2 of the plan in the introduction.

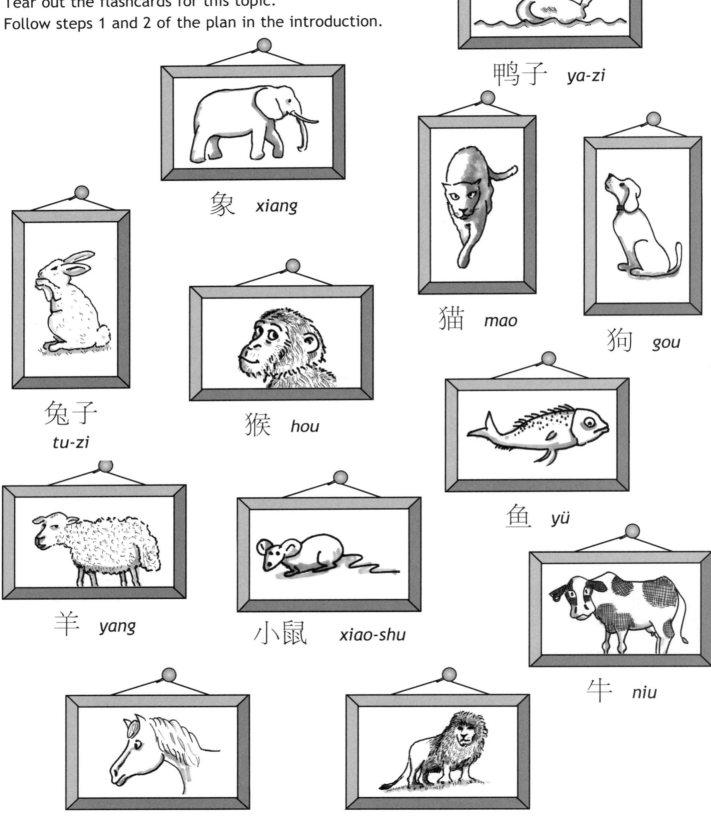

鸭子 *ya-zi*

象 *xiang*

猫 *mao*

狗 *gou*

兔子
tu-zi

猴 *hou*

鱼 *yü*

羊 *yang*

小鼠 *xiao-shu*

牛 *niu*

马 *ma*

狮子 *shi-zi*

◎ **M**atch the animals to their associated pictures, as in the example.

马　　　　　　兔子　　　　　　　　猫

　　猴　　　　　　　　　　　狗

　羊　　　小鼠

牛　　　狮子　　　　　　　鱼

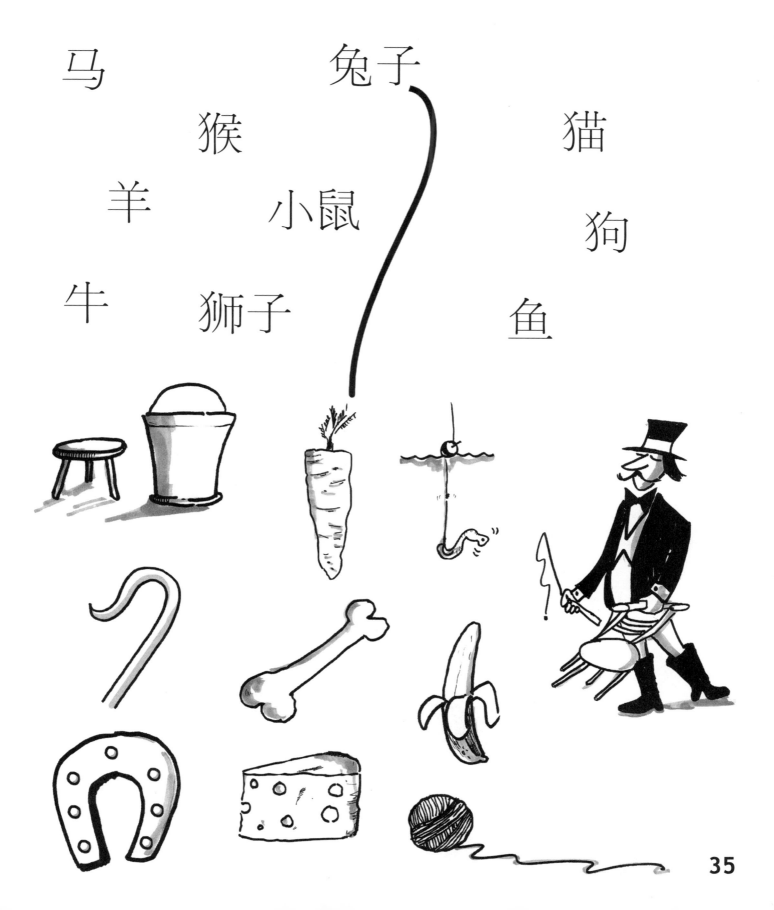

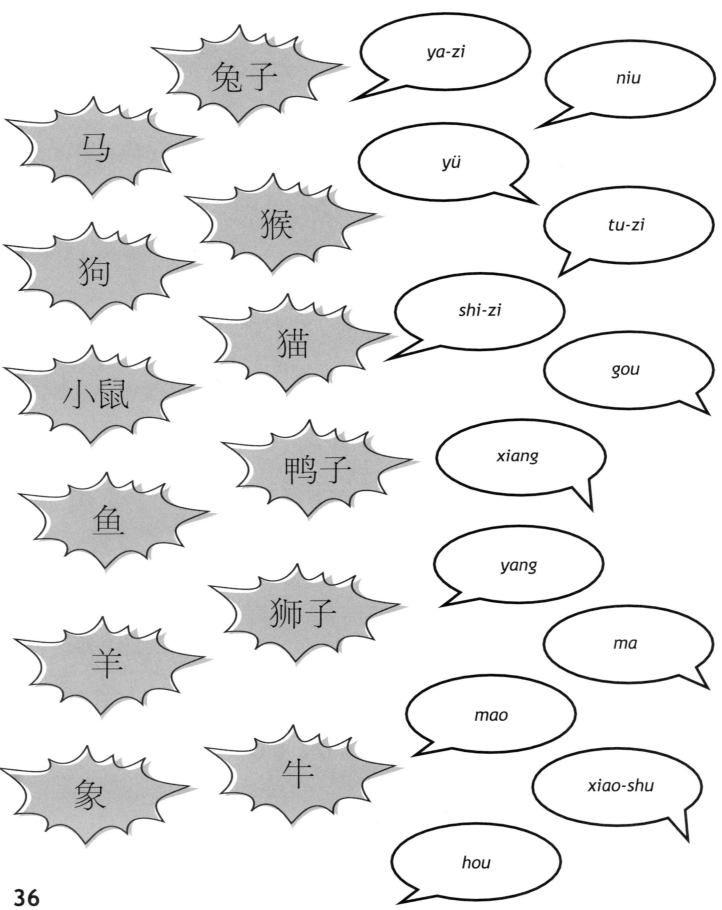

Check (✔) the animal words you can find in the word pile.

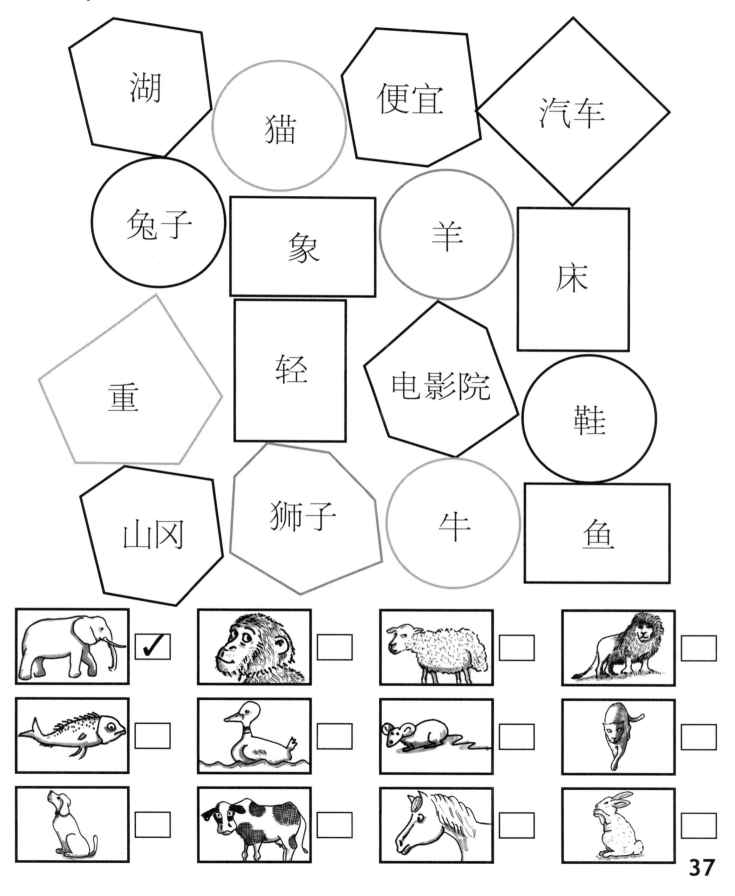

Join the Chinese animals to their English equivalents.

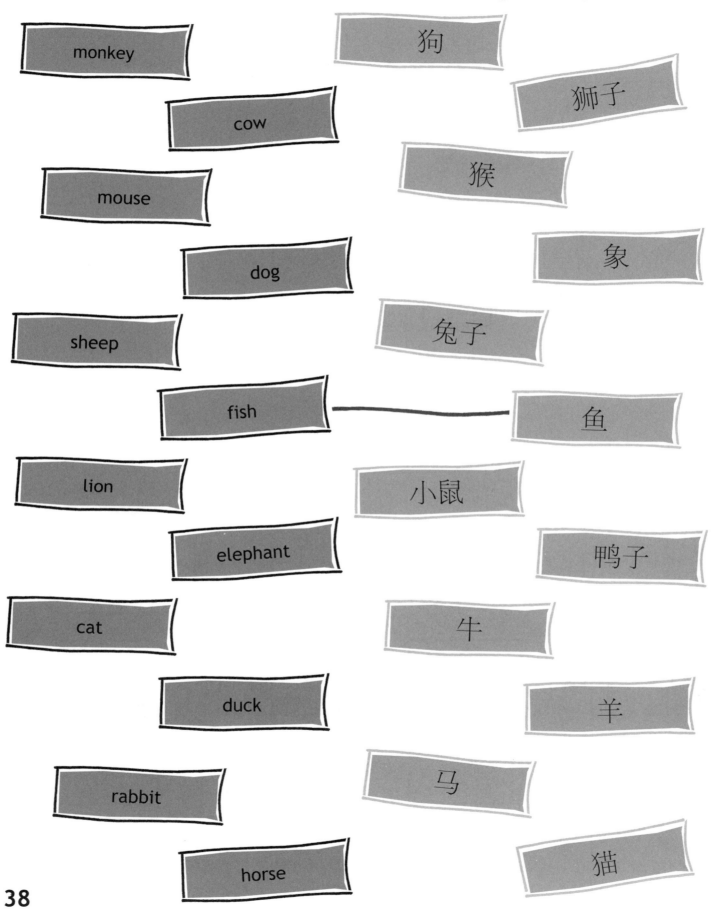

monkey

狗

狮子

cow

猴

mouse

象

dog

兔子

sheep

fish ——— 鱼

lion

小鼠

elephant

鸭子

cat

牛

duck

羊

rabbit

马

horse

猫

❼ PARTS OF THE BODY

Look at the pictures of parts of the body.
Tear out the flashcards for this topic.
Follow steps 1 and 2 of the plan in the introduction.

手指
shou-zhi

头 *tou*

胳膊
ge-bo

眼睛 *yan-jing*

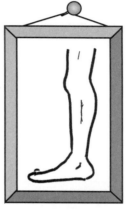

腿 *tui*

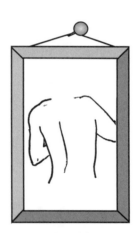

脊背
ji-bei

手 *shou*

头发 *tou-fa*

肚子
du-zi

耳朵 *er-duo*

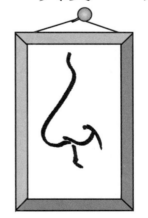

鼻子
bi-zi

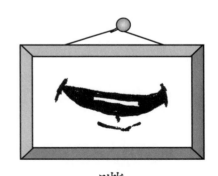

嘴
zui

39

Someone has ripped up the Chinese words for parts of the body. Can you join the two halves of the word again?

⊚ **S**ee if you can find and circle six parts of the body in the word square, then draw them in the boxes below.

脊	车	嘴	汽	干	门	共	院
橱	连	子	狗	快	田	林	太
帽	重	冈	山	好	鱼	农	头
马	湖	山	新	旧	小	河	发
餐	兔	腿	狮	路	衫	衬	慢
耳	炉	电	出	店	不	谢	火
朵	天	对	子	鼻	子	户	今
天	里	眼	睛	今	火	那	明

The words can run left to right, or top to bottom:

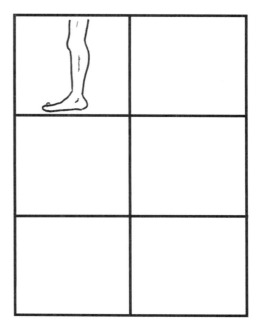

⊚ **N**ow match the Chinese to the pronunciation.

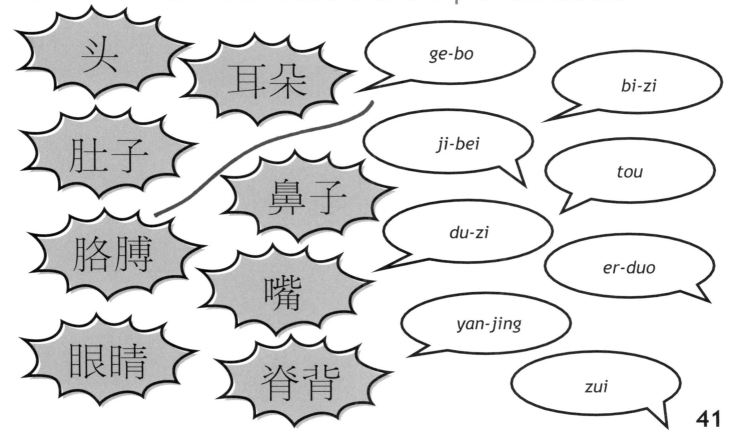

头　　耳朵　　ge-bo　　bi-zi

肚子　　ji-bei　　tou

胳膊　　鼻子　　du-zi　　er-duo

嘴　　yan-jing

眼睛　　脊背　　zui

41

◎ Label the body with the correct number, and write the pronunciation next to the words.

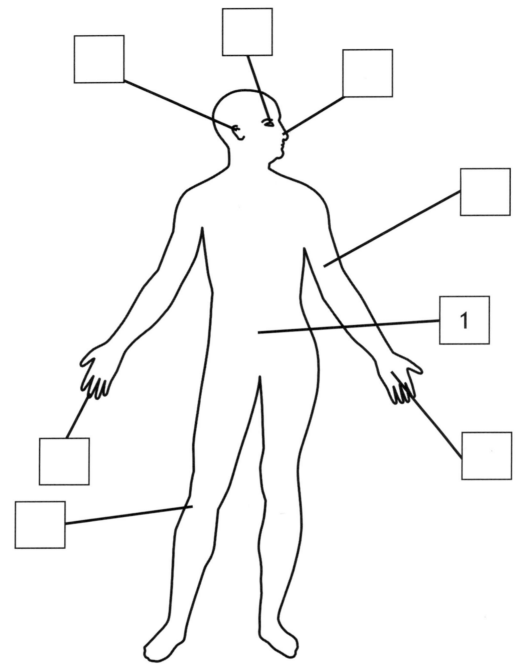

1 肚子 *du-zi*_____   2 胳膊 _____

3 鼻子 _____   4 手 _____

5 耳朵 _____   6 腿 _____

7 眼睛 _____   8 手指 _____

Finally, match the Chinese words, their pronunciation, and the English meanings, as in the example.

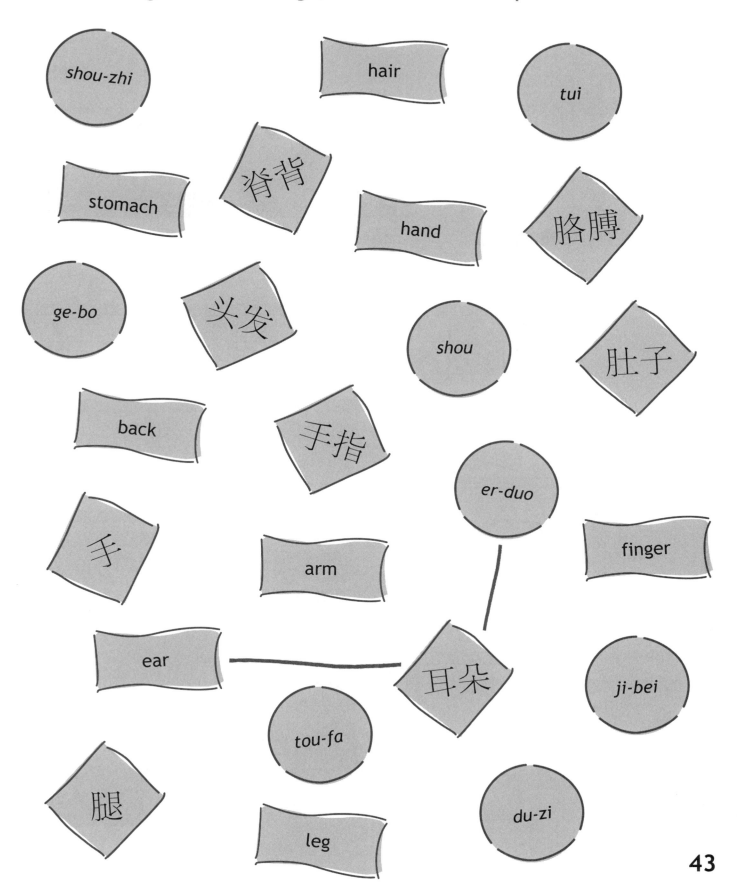

shou-zhi

hair

tui

脊背

stomach

胳膊

hand

ge-bo

头发

shou

肚子

back

手指

er-duo

手

arm

finger

ear

耳朵

ji-bei

tou-fa

腿

leg

du-zi

43

Look at the pictures.
Tear out the flashcards for this topic.
Follow steps 1 and 2 of the plan in the introduction.

哪里? *na-li*

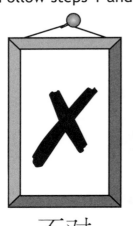

不对

bu-dui

对 *dui*

你好 *ni-hao*

再见

zai-jian

昨天 *zuo-tian*

今天 *jin-tian*

明天 *ming-tian*

这里
zhe-li

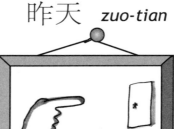

那里 *na-li*

现在 *xian-zai*

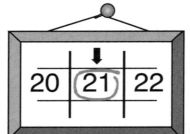

多少?

duo-shao

对不起！

dui-bu-qi

太好了！

tai-hao-le

请 *qing*

谢谢 *xie-xie*

Match the Chinese words to their English equivalents.

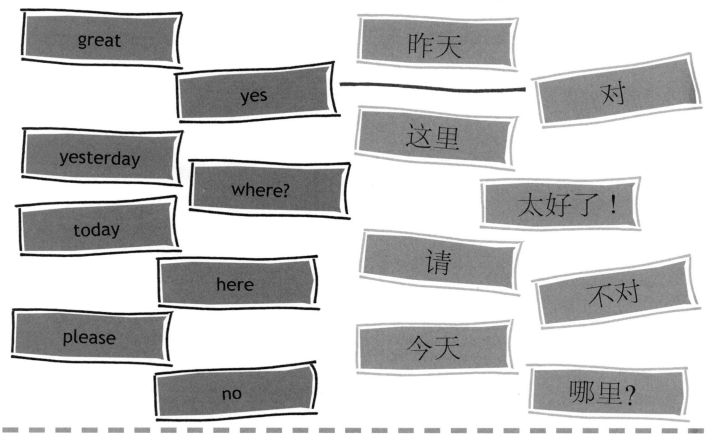

Now match the Chinese to the pronunciation.

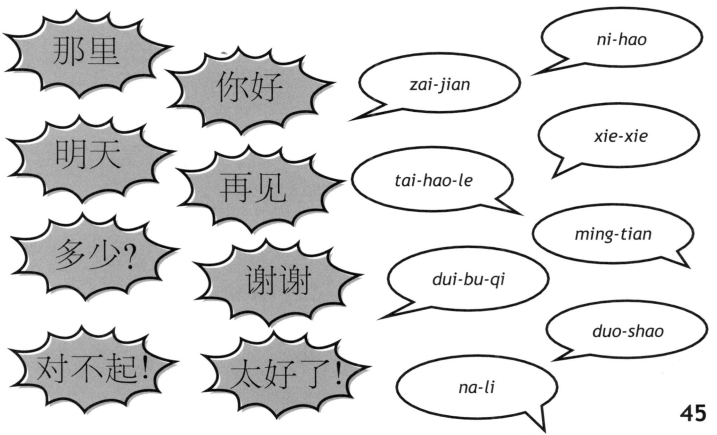

Choose the Chinese word that matches the picture to fill in the English word at the bottom of the page.

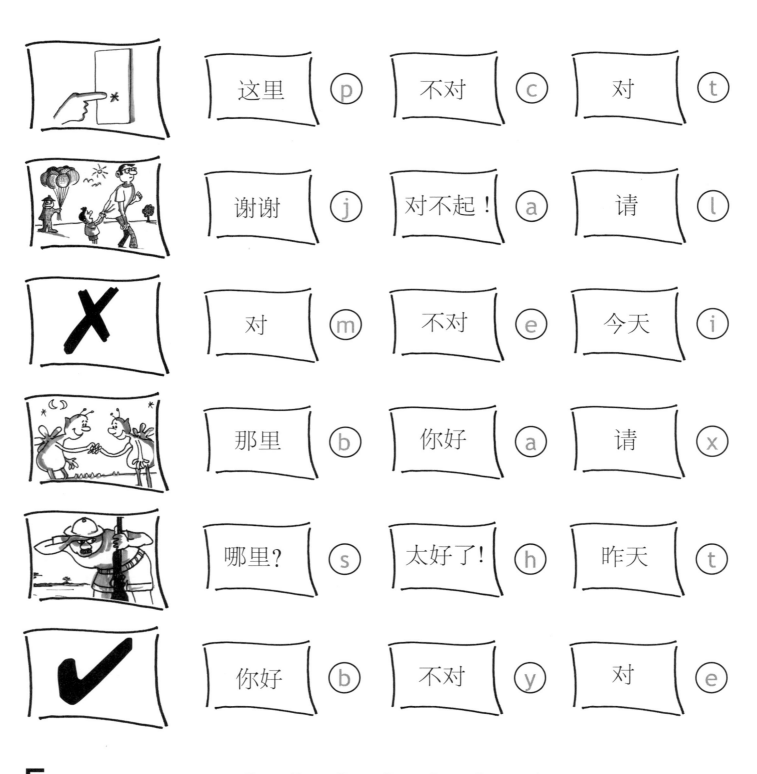

这里 (p)	不对 (c)	对 (t)
谢谢 (j)	对不起！(a)	请 (l)
对 (m)	不对 (e)	今天 (i)
那里 (b)	你好 (a)	请 (x)
哪里？(s)	太好了! (h)	昨天 (t)
你好 (b)	不对 (y)	对 (e)

English word: (p) ◯ ◯ ◯ ◯ ◯

What are these people saying? Write the correct number in each speech bubble, as in the example.

1. 你好　　2. 请　　　3. 对　　　4. 不对

5. 这里　　6. 对不起!　7. 哪里?　　8. 多少?

◎ **F**inally, match the Chinese words, their pronunciation, and the English meanings, as in the example.

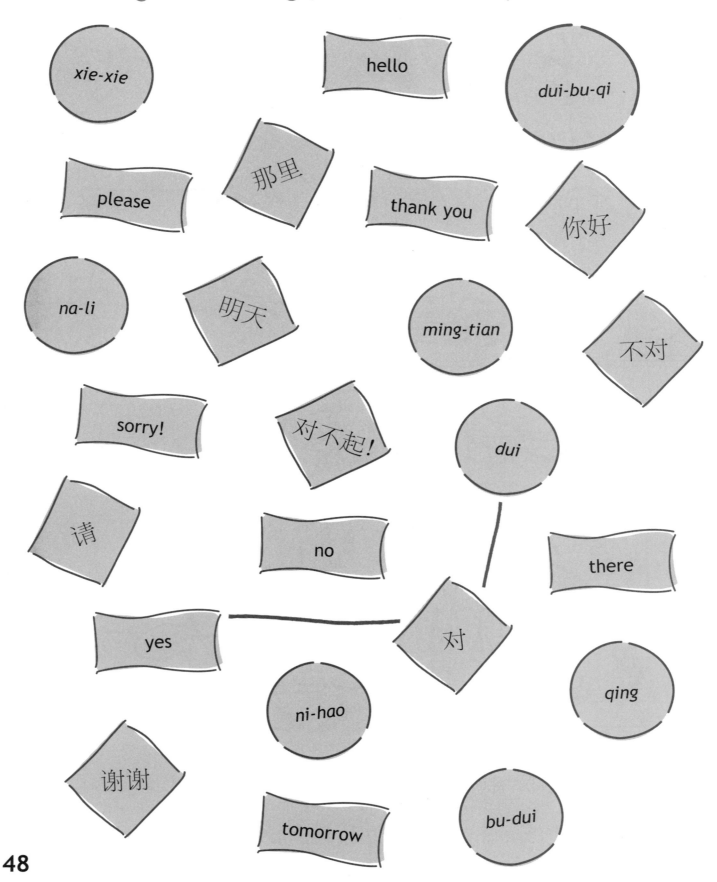

xie-xie

hello

dui-bu-qi

please

那里

thank you

你好

na-li

明天

ming-tian

不对

sorry!

对不起!

dui

请

no

there

yes

对

qing

ni-hao

谢谢

tomorrow

bu-dui

● ROUND-UP

This section is designed to review all the 100 words you have met in the different topics. It is a good idea to test yourself with your flashcards before trying this section.

◎ These ten objects are hidden in the picture. Can you find and circle them?

门　　　花　　　床　　　大衣　　　帽子

自行车　　椅子　　　狗　　　鱼　　　袜子

◎ **S**ee if you can remember all these words.

今天

公共汽车

快

鼻子

沙漠

对

橱柜

狮子

连衣裙

便宜

河

腿

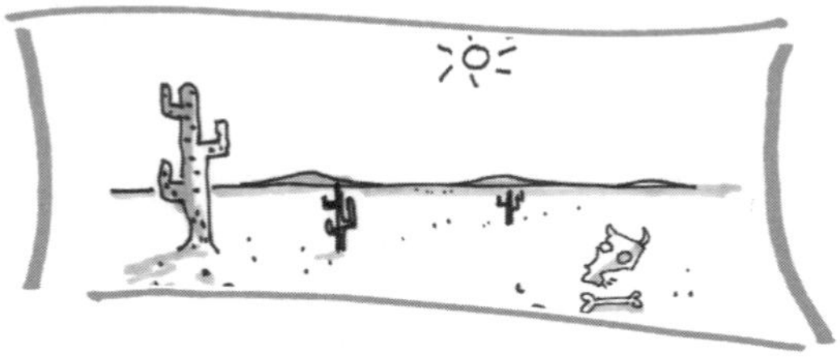

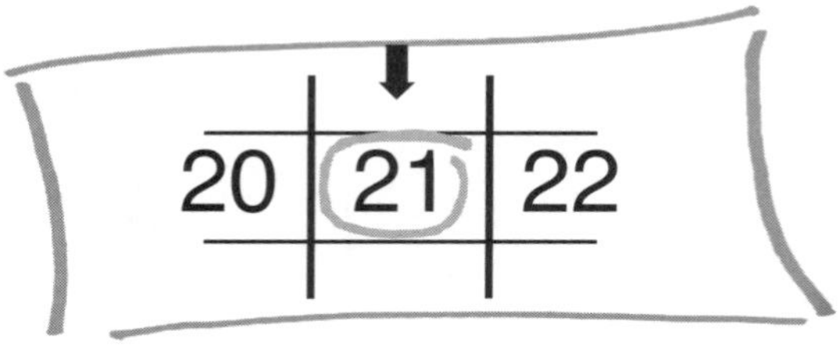

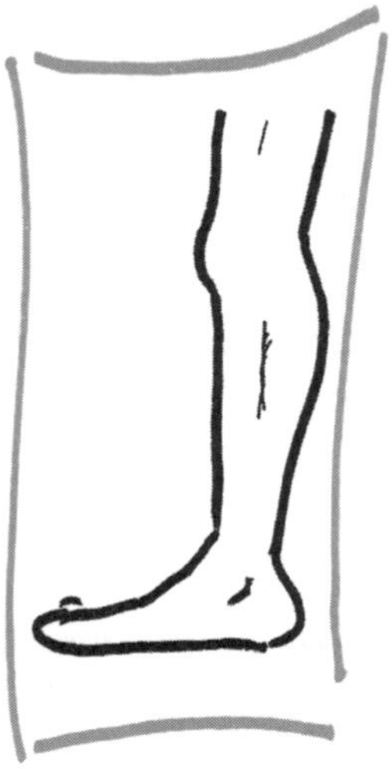

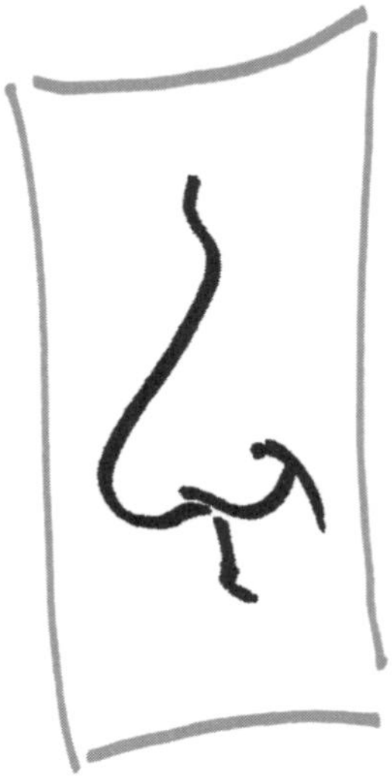

◎ **F**ind the odd one out in these groups of words and say why.

| 狗 | 牛 | 桌子 | 猴 |

Because it isn't an animal.

| 汽车 | 公共汽车 | 火车 | 电话 |

| 农场 | 大衣 | 衬衫 | 裙子 |

| 海 | 湖 | 河 | 树 |

| 贵 | 脏 | 干净 | 电影院 |

| 兔子 | 猫 | 鱼 | 狮子 |

| 胳膊 | 沙发 | 头 | 肚子 |

| 请 | 昨天 | 明天 | 今天 |

| 炉子 | 床 | 橱柜 | 电冰箱 |

○ **L**ook at the objects below for 30 seconds.

○ **C**over the picture and try to remember all the objects.
Circle the Chinese words for those you remember.

花   鞋   谢谢   门

汽车 不对   这里   大衣   火车

皮带   山   椅子   马

袜子   T-恤衫   眼睛   床

短裤   出租车   电视机   猴

Now match the Chinese words, their pronunciation, and the English meanings, as in the example.

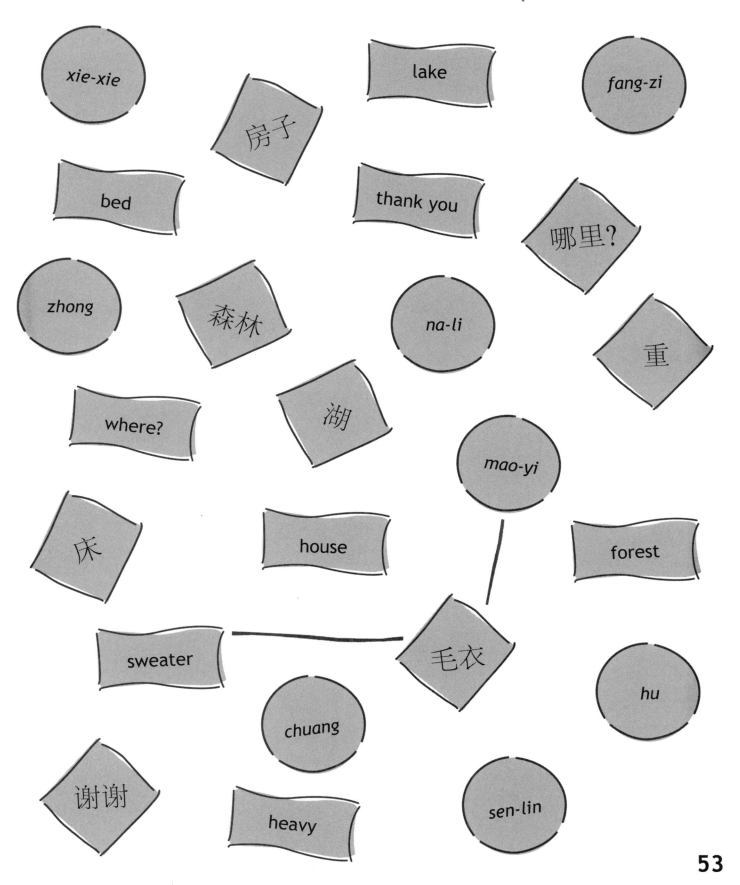

xie-xie

房子

lake

fang-zi

bed

thank you

哪里?

zhong

森林

na-li

重

where?

湖

mao-yi

床

house

forest

sweater

毛衣

hu

chuang

谢谢

heavy

sen-lin

◎ **F**ill in the English phrase at the bottom of the page.

沙发 (w)	出租车 (g)	耳朵 (t)
大衣 (o)	脏 (a)	桥 (e)
对 (m)	多少? (l)	今天 (i)
牛 (b)	窗户 (l)	餐馆 (h)
哪里? (e)	嘴 (a)	狗 (d)
眼睛 (o)	桌子 (p)	你好 (v)
山冈 (n)	不对 (y)	公共汽车 (r)
兔子 (n)	道路 (e)	炉子 (s)

54 **E**nglish phrase: (w) ( ) ( ) ( ) ( ) ( ) ( ) !

Look at the two pictures and check (✔) the objects that are different in Picture B.

Picture A

Picture B

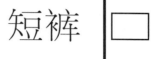 短裤 ☐

 T-恤衫 ☐

 门 ☐

 猫 ☐

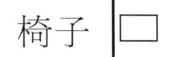 椅子 ☐

 鱼 ☐

 袜子 ☐

 狗 ☐

Now join the Chinese words to their English equivalents.

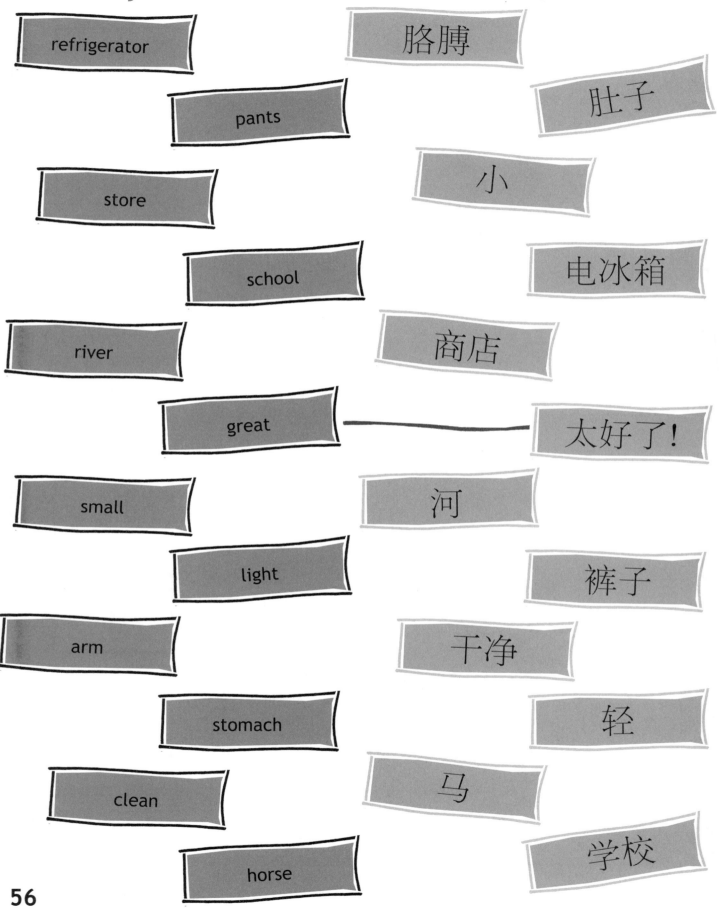

refrigerator

胳膊

pants

肚子

store

小

school

电冰箱

river

商店

great ———— 太好了!

small

河

light

裤子

arm

干净

stomach

轻

clean

马

horse

学校

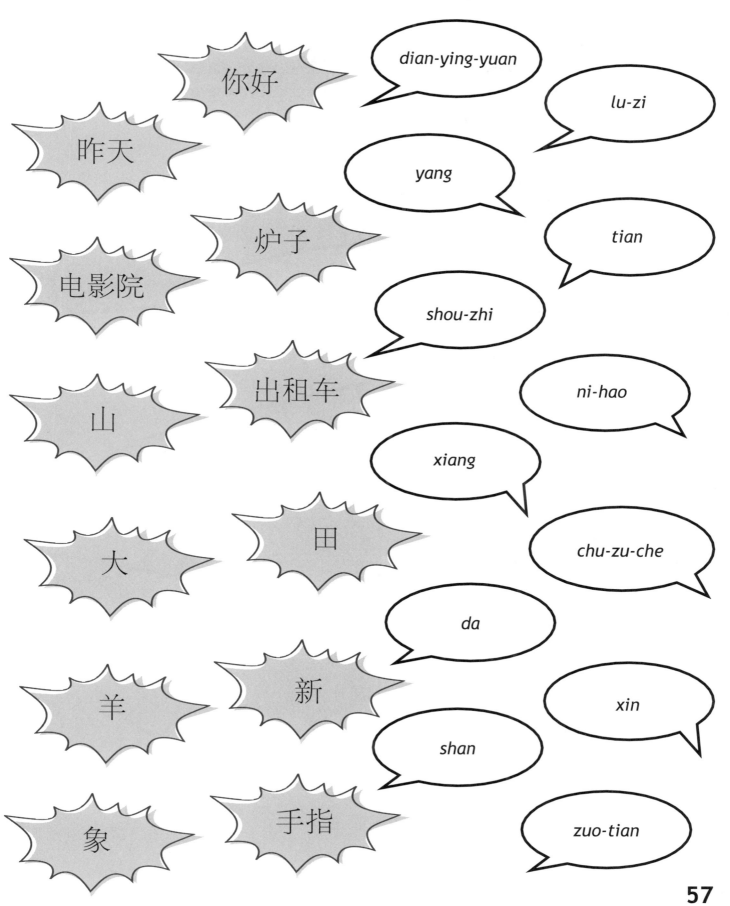

◎ Snake game.

● You will need a die and counter(s). You can challenge yourself to reach the finish or play with someone else. You have to throw the exact number to finish.

● Throw the die and move forward that number of spaces. When you land on a word you must pronounce it and say what it means in English. If you can't, you have to go back to the square you came from.

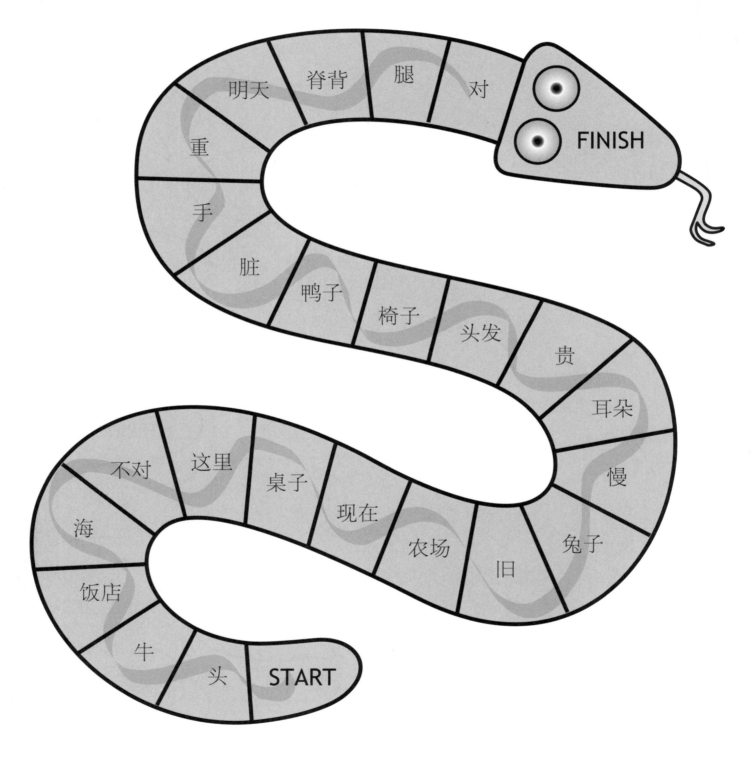

◎ Answers

❶ Around the home

Page 10 (top)

See page 9 for correct picture.

Page 10 (bottom)

door	门
cupboard	橱柜
stove	炉子
bed	床
table	桌子
chair	椅子
refrigerator	电冰箱
computer	电脑

Page 11 (top)

桌子	*zhuo-zi*
橱柜	*chu-gui*
电脑	*dian-nao*
床	*chuang*
窗户	*chuang-hu*
电话	*dian-hua*
电视机	*dian-shi-ji*
椅子	*yi-zi*

Page 11 (bottom)

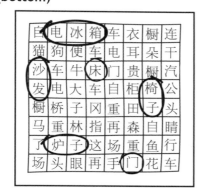

Page 12

Page 13

English word: window

❷ Clothes

Page 15 (top)

连衣裙	*lian-yi-qün*
短裤	*duan-ku*
鞋	*xie*
皮带	*pi-dai*
衬衫	*chen-shan*
T-恤衫	*ti-xü-shan*
帽子	*mao-zi*
袜子	*wa-zi*

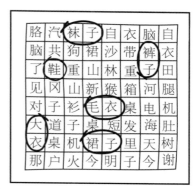

Page 15 (bottom)

Page 16

hat	帽子	*mao-zi*
shoe	鞋	*xie*
sock	袜子	*wa-zi*
shorts	短裤	*duan-ku*
t-shirt	T-恤衫	*ti-xü-shan*
belt	皮带	*pi-dai*
coat	大衣	*da-yi*
pants	裤子	*ku-zi*

Page 17

帽子 (hat)	2
大衣 (coat)	0
皮带 (belt)	2
鞋 (shoe)	2
裤子 (pants)	0
短裤 (shorts)	2
连衣裙 (dress)	1
袜子 (sock)	6 (3 pairs)
裙子 (skirt)	1
T-恤衫 (t-shirt)	3
衬衫 (shirt)	0
毛衣 (sweater)	1

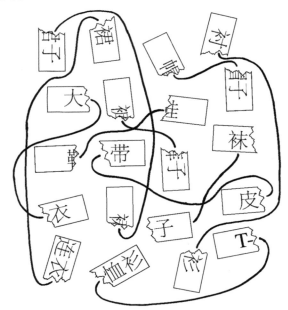

③ AROUND TOWN

Page 20 (top)

movie theater	电影院
store	商店
hotel	饭店
taxi	出租车
car	汽车
train	火车
school	学校
house	房子

Page 20 (bottom)

bicycle	4
taxi	7
house	2
train	6
bus	1
road	3
car	5

Page 21

学校   出租车   公共汽车

汽车   火车   餐馆

饭店   自行车

Page 22

English word: school

Page 23

公共汽车	*gong-gong-qi-che*
出租汽车	*chu-zu-che*
学校	*xüe-xiao*
汽车	*qi-che*
饭店	*fan-dian*
房子	*fang-zi*
自行车	*zi-xing-che*
火车	*huo-che*
商店	*shang-dian*
电影院	*dian-ying-yuan*
餐馆	*can-guan*
道路	*dao-lu*

④ COUNTRYSIDE

Page 25

See page 24 for correct picture.

Page 26

桥	✔	田	✔
树	✔	森林	✔
沙漠	✘	湖	✘
山冈	✘	河	✔
山	✔	花	✔
海	✘	农场	✔

Page 27 (top)

山	*shan*
河	*he*
森林	*sen-lin*
沙漠	*sha-mo*
海	*hai*
农场	*nong-chang*
桥	*qiao*
田	*tian*

Page 27 (bottom)

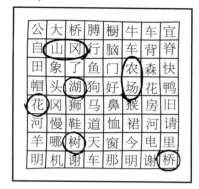

Page 28

sea	海	*hai*
lake	湖	*hu*
desert	沙漠	*sha-mo*
farm	农场	*nong-chang*
flower	花	*hua*
mountain	山	*shan*
river	河	*he*
field	田	*tian*

❺ OPPOSITES

Page 30

expensive	贵
big	大
light	轻
slow	慢
clean	干净
inexpensive	便宜
dirty	脏
small	小
heavy	重
new	新
fast	快
old	旧

Page 31

English word: change

Page 32

Odd one outs are those which are not opposites:

重
小
新
脏
慢
便宜

Page 33

old	新
big	大
new	旧
slow	快
dirty	干净
small	小
heavy	轻
clean	脏
light	重
expensive	便宜
inexpensive	贵

❻ ANIMALS

Page 35

牛　　兔子　　鱼　　狮子

羊　　狗　　猴

马　　小鼠　　猫

Page 36

兔子	*tu-zi*
马	*ma*
猴	*hou*
狗	*gou*
猫	*mao*
小鼠	*xiao-shu*
鸭子	*ya-zi*
鱼	*yü*
狮子	*shi-zi*
羊	*yang*
牛	*niu*
象	*xiang*

Page 37

elephant	✔	mouse	✘
monkey	✘	cat	✔
sheep	✔	dog	✘
lion	✔	cow	✔
fish	✔	horse	✘
duck	✘	rabbit	✔

Page 38

monkey	猴
cow	牛
mouse	小鼠
dog	狗
sheep	羊
fish	鱼
lion	狮子
elephant	象
cat	猫
duck	鸭子
rabbit	兔子
horse	马

❼ PARTS OF THE BODY

Page 40

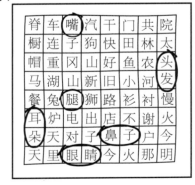

Page 41 (top)

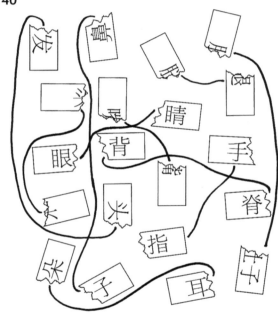

You should have also drawn pictures of:

leg; mouth; ear; nose; eye; hair

Page 41 (bottom)

头	*tou*
耳朵	*er-duo*
肚子	*du-zi*
鼻子	*bi-zi*
胳膊	*ge-bo*
嘴	*zui*
眼睛	*yan-jing*
脊背	*ji-bei*

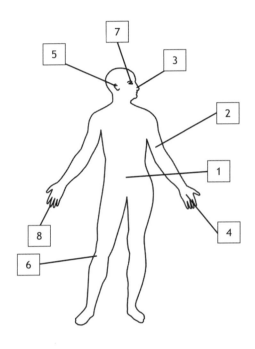

Page 42

1.	肚子	*du-zi*
2.	胳膊	*ge-bo*
3.	鼻子	*bi-zi*
4.	手	*shou*
5.	耳朵	*er-duo*
6.	腿	*tui*
7.	眼睛	*yan-jing*
8.	手指	*shou-zhi*

Page 43

ear	耳朵	*er-duo*
hair	头发	*tou-fa*
hand	手	*shou*
stomach	肚子	*du-zi*
arm	胳膊	*ge-bo*
back	脊背	*ji-bei*
finger	手指	*shou-zhi*
leg	腿	*tui*

⑧ USEFUL EXPRESSIONS

Page 45 (top)

great	太好了！
yes	对
yesterday	昨天
where?	哪里?
today	今天
here	这里
please	请
no	不对

Page 45 (bottom)

那里	*na-li*
你好	*ni-hao*
明天	*ming-tian*
再见	*zai-jian*
多少?	*duo-sha*
谢谢	*xie-xie*
对不起！	*dui-bu-qi*
太好了！	*tai-hao-le*

Page 46

English word: please

Page 47

Page 48

yes	对	*dui*
hello	你好	*ni-hao*
no	不对	*bu-dui*
sorry!	对不起！	*dui-bu-qi*
please	请	*qing*
there	那里	*na-li*
thank you	谢谢	*xie-xie*
tomorrow	明天	*ming-tian*

● ROUND-UP

Page 49

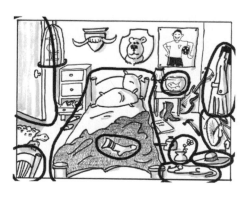

Page 50

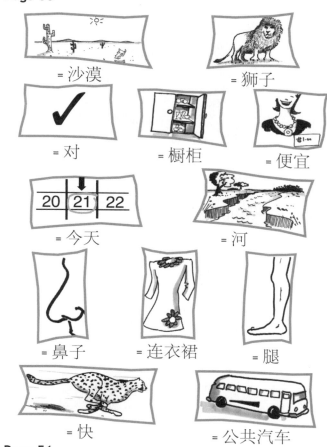

= 沙漠

= 狮子

= 对

= 橱柜

= 便宜

= 今天

= 河

= 鼻子

= 连衣裙

= 腿

= 快

= 公共汽车

Page 51

桌子 (Because it isn't an animal.)
电话 (Because it isn't a means of transportation.)
农场 (Because it isn't an item of clothing.)
树 (Because it isn't connected with water.)
电影院 (Because it isn't a descriptive word.)
鱼 (Because it lives in water/doesn't have legs.)
沙发 (Because it isn't a part of the body.)
请 (Because it isn't an expression of time.)
床 (Because you wouldn't find it in the kitchen.)

Page 52

Words that appear in the picture:

T-恤衫
汽车
花
鞋
火车
猴
电视机
椅子
皮带
短裤

Page 53

sweater	毛衣	*mao-yi*
lake	湖	*hu*
thank you	谢谢	*xie-xie*
bed	床	*chuang*
house	房子	*fang-zi*
forest	森林	*sen-lin*
where?	哪里?	*na-li*
heavy	重	*zhong*

Page 54

English phrase: well done!

Page 55

短裤	✔ (shade)
T-恤衫	✘
门	✔ (handle)
猫	✘
椅子	✔ (back)
鱼	✔ (direction)
袜子	✔ (pattern)
狗	✘

Page 56

refrigerator	电冰箱
pants	裤子
store	商店
school	学校
river	河
great!	太好了！
small	小
light	轻
arm	胳膊
stomach	肚子
clean	干净
horse	马

Page 57

你好	*ni-hao*
昨天	*zuo-tian*
炉子	*lu-zi*
电影院	*dian-ying-yuan*
出租车	*chu-zu-che*
山	*shan*
田	*tian*
大	*da*
新	*xin*
羊	*yang*
手指	*shou-zhi*
象	*xiang*

Page 58

Here are the English equivalents of the word, in order from START to FINISH:

head *tou*	farm *nong-chang*	duck *ya-zi*
cow *niu*	old *jiu*	dirty *zang*
hotel *fan-dian*	rabbit *tu-zi*	hand *shou*
sea *hai*	slow *man*	heavy *zhong*
no *bu-dui*	ear *er-duo*	tomorrow *ming-tian*
here *zhe-li*	expensive *gui*	back *ji-bei*
table *zhuo-zi*	hair *tou-fa*	leg *tui*
now *shian-ziai*	chair *yi-zi*	yes *dui*

电脑

dian-nao

窗户

chuang-hu

桌子

zhuo-zi

橱柜

chu-gui

电冰箱

dian-bing-xiang

椅子

yi-zi

沙发

sha-fa

炉子

lu-zi

门

men

床

chuang

电话

dian-hua

电视机

dian-shi-ji

window	computer
cupboard	table
chair	refrigerator
stove	sofa
bed	door
television	telephone

皮带

pi-dai

大衣

da-yi

裙子

qün-zi

帽子

mao-zi

T-恤衫

ti-xü-shan

鞋

xie

毛衣

mao-yi

衬衫

chen-shan

短裤

duan-ku

袜子

wa-zi

裤子

ku-zi

连衣裙

lian-yi-qün

coat	belt
hat	skirt
shoe	t-shirt
shirt	sweater
sock	shorts
dress	pants

学校
xüe-xiao

汽车
qi-che

道路
dao-lu

电影院
dian-ying-yuan

饭店
fan-dian

商店
shang-dian

出租车
chu-zu-che

自行车
zi-xing-che

餐馆
can-guan

公共汽车
gong-gong-qi-che

火车
huo-che

房子
fang-zi

car	school
movie theater	road
store	hotel
bicycle	taxi
bus	restaurant
house	train

湖
hu

森林
sen-lin

山冈
shan-gang

海
hai

山
shan

树
shu

沙漠
sha-mo

花
hua

桥
qiao

河
he

农场
nong-chang

田
tian

forest	lake
sea	hill
tree	mountain
flower	desert
river	bridge
field	farm

重
zhong

轻
qing

大
da

小
xiao

旧
jiu

新
xin

快
kuai

慢
man

干净
gan-jing

脏
zang

便宜
pian-yi

贵
gui

xiang

yang

finger	arm
mouth	head
leg	ear
stomach	hand
hair	eye
back	nose

请
qing

谢谢
xie-xie

对
dui

不对
bu-dui

你好
ni-hao

再见
zai-jian

昨天
zuo-tian

今天
jin-tian

明天
ming-tian

哪里？
na-li

这里
zhe-li

那里
na-li

对不起！
dui-bu-qi

多少？
duo-shao

太好了！
tai-hao-le

现在
xian-zai

thank you	please
no	yes
goodbye	hello
today	yesterday
where?	tomorrow
there	here
how much?	sorry!
now	great!